The Let's Talk Library™

Let's Talk About When Your Mom or Dad Is Unhappy

Diana Star Helmer

A HAZELDEN / PowerKids Press™ Book

Published in 1999 by The Rosen Publishing Group, Inc.
29 East 21st Street, New York, NY 10010

This edition published in 1999 by Hazelden
PO Box 176, Center City, MN 55012-0176

Copyright © 1999 by The Rosen Publishing Group, Inc.

First Edition

Book Design: Erin McKenna

Photo Credits and Illustrations: p. 4 by Thomas Mangieri; pp. 7, 8, 12, 19 by Bonnie Rothstein Brewer; pp. 11, 16, 20 © Skjold Photographs; p. 15 by Seth Dinnerman.

Helmer, Diana Star.
    Let's talk about when your mom or dad is unhappy / by Diana Star Helmer.
        p.   cm. — (The let's talk library)
    Includes index.
    Summary: Explains the difference between being sad and being clinically depressed and discusses ways a child can deal with having a parent who is sad or depressed.
    ISBN 1-56838-277-4
    1. Parents—Psychology—Juvenile literature. 2. Parents—Mental health—Juvenile literature. 3. Sadness—Juvenile literature. 4. Depression, Mental—Juvenile literature. 5. Parent and child—Juvenile literature. [1. Sadness. 2. Depression, Mental.] I. Title. II. Series
HQ755.8.H34   1998
155.4'124—dc21   98-11548
                                                                      CIP
                                                                       AC

Manufactured in the United States of America

Table of Contents

What Happened?

"Hi, Dad!" Larry said. Larry and his friend Quinn came into the house after school.

"Oh, hi," Larry's dad said. "Listen, I need you guys to be quiet today. Okay?" Then he left.

"Your dad always talks and jokes with me," Quinn whispered. "But he sounds sad today. Did you do something bad?"

"I don't know what's wrong," Larry said. "He sounds that way when he's thinking hard or worrying about his job. Or he's just tired."

◀ We may not always know why a parent is sad. But talking to a friend about how you feel can help you.

Nobody's Fault

Everyone feels sad sometimes. You may have been sad when you couldn't see a friend. Or maybe you lost something. Or you tried hard at school but still didn't understand the work. There are many reasons why a kid might feel sad. There are many reasons why a grown-up might feel sad too. Grown-ups miss their friends, lose things, and want to do better in their work too. If your mom or dad is sad, it doesn't mean you did something wrong. After all, when you're sad, it usually doesn't mean your parents did something wrong, does it?

If a parent wants to be alone, that ▶ might be a sign that he is sad.

Thinking About Next Time

When one of your parents is sad, thinking about a time when you were sad can help you understand your parent's feelings. Maybe you were sad because you didn't win a race at school. If you think about that race, you might remember that you tried your best. You might remember what the winner did differently. You could think of ways to do better in the next race.

Sometimes finding a quiet place where you can be alone to think can help you if you're sad. This can also help a sad grown-up.

◀ Letting a parent have some quiet time can help her sort out her feelings.

Everyone Gets Grumpy

Sometimes sad people don't act sad. They act **grumpy** (GRUM-pee) instead. A grumpy person can say the wrong thing and make you feel bad. But you don't have to let that person ruin your day. You can stay calm when your mom is acting grumpy. Remember, it's not your fault that your parent is grumpy.

What can you do if your parent is acting sad or grumpy? You could try going into a different room for a little while. Or you and your parent can have quiet time together.

Quiet time between you and your parent ▶
can make both of you feel better.

Should I Worry?

Often, grown-ups don't want kids to worry about them. If your mom or dad is feeling sad, he or she may not say why. But kids worry about their parents anyway. Sometimes, if you're sad, your parents can't make you feel happy. Instead, you have to feel better on your own. It's important to understand that you can't always make your sad mom or dad feel better. Give your parent time to work things out alone. Your dad or mom knows that you are there to help if he or she needs you. That's what families and friends do. They take turns helping each other.

◄ Everyone in the family can help with household chores if someone is feeling sad.

Eating, Sleeping, Exercise

Sometimes people get so busy they may not eat or sleep enough. A person's body gets tired without these things. A body also needs **exercise** (EK-sur-syz) to stay healthy. It can get out of shape without it. When your body is tired and out of shape, you may feel bored and sad. You can help a sad person who may be having trouble with eating or sleeping by talking to an adult that you trust. He or she can talk to the person who is sad and try to get help for that person.

Exercise is more important than you think. Not only is it good for your body, it's also good for your mind! ▶

A Big Sadness

Pam noticed that her mom had been sad for a long time. She went to talk to her dad.

"Your mom has been sad because she has a sickness called **depression** (dih-PREH-shun)," Dad said.

"Like the flu or a cold?" Pam asked. "Why doesn't Mom's sickness go away?"

Depression is tricky. It can mean being a little sad. But it can also be a big sadness that can last a long time.

◀ You can talk to an adult if you want to know more about depression.

A Sickness Without Spots

Depression is a sneaky sickness. There are no fevers or spots when you have depression. So how do you know if someone is just a little sad, or if she has depression?

Someone with depression may eat or sleep more or less than before. Someone with depression is usually sad for two weeks or longer, and she might not even know why she's sad. Things that used to make her happy don't make her happy anymore. Also, depressed people don't feel like doing very much.

A person with depression may have to take long naps or rest in bed a lot. ▶

Everyone Needs Help Sometimes

Sometimes sicknesses like depression last a short time. Sometimes they last for years. A person with depression needs help, just like any person who is ill. Doctors try to make sure a depressed person is getting good food, enough sleep, and exercise. If that doesn't help, some people take **medicine** (MEH-dih-sin) for their depression. The medicine can help people stop feeling sad. Other people can learn to change their sad feelings by talking about those feelings. A trained person who listens to other people's feelings is called a **therapist** (THER-uh-pist).

◀ Exercise can be helpful for a person who's depressed. And exercising with a friend can be even better.

Somebody Loves You

Sarah's mom had been depressed. Sarah didn't know what to do for her mom. But one day after school, Sarah's mom greeted her in the kitchen.

"I went to the doctor today," her mom said. "I'm trying new ways to feel better."

"I'm glad," Sarah said. "I hate it when you're sad."

"I hate it, too," Mom said. "And I know it can be hard for you. But you help me just by loving me."

"I can do that!" said Sarah as she hugged her mom.

Glossary

depression (dih-PREH-shun) A sickness where a person is very sad for a long time. The sadness makes it hard for the person to work or play.

exercise (EK-sur-syz) Running, swimming, biking, and other activities that use different parts of your body.

grumpy (GRUM-pee) Feeling bad or grouchy.

medicine (MEH-dih-sin) A drug given by a doctor that makes a sick person feel better.

therapist (THER-uh-pist) A person who is trained to work with people to help them figure out their feelings.

Index